Quiet Moments
in the
GARDEN

Compiled by
H. Norman Wright

Illustrated by
Stacie Merlo

HARVEST HOUSE PUBLISHERS
Eugene, Oregon 97402

Unless otherwise indicated, text is written by H. Norman Wright.
Artwork by Stacie Merlo.

QUIET MOMENTS IN THE GARDEN

Copyright © 1997 by Harvest House Publishers
Eugene, Oregon 97402

ISBN 1-56507-530-7

Designed by Koechel Peterson & Associates, Minneapolis, Minnesota.

Printed in Mexico.

97 98 99 00 01 02 03 04 05 06 / DR / 10 9 8 7 6 5 4 3 2 1

To:

Clare M Grupp

From:

Kathryn E Grupp

On:

Christmas 1997

What Is a Garden?

What is a garden?

A garden is a place of solitude, a retreat which provides refreshment.

The silent beauty of a garden lifts the weariness of a tired body and a troubled mind.

A garden brings into the viewer's life a sense of wholeness and harmony, especially the harmony of color.

Awake, O north wind; and come, thou south; blow upon my garden, that the spices thereof may flow out. Let my beloved come into his garden, and eat his pleasant fruits.

THE SONG OF SOLOMON

My heart shall be thy garden.
Come, my own,
Into thy garden; thine be happy hours
Among my fairest thoughts, my tallest
flowers,
From root to crowning petal thine alone.

ALICE MEYNELL

What is a Garden?

To one it is a piece of ground
For which some gravel must be found.
To some, those seeds that must be sown,
To some a lawn that must be mown.
To some a ton of Cheddar rocks;

To some, who dare not pick a flower–
A man, at eighteen pence an hour.
To some, it is a silly jest
About the latest garden pest;
To some, a haven where they find
Forgetfulness and peace of mind....

REGINALD ARKELL

Perhaps the chiefest attraction of a garden is that occupation can always be found there...with mind and fingers busy, cares are soon forgotten.

ALICIA AMHERST

Apart from Thee we plant in vain
The root and sow the seed;
Thy early and Thy later rain,
Thy sun and dew we need.

JOHN GREENLEAF WHITTIER

Adam was a gardener, and God
who made him sees
That half a proper gardener's work is
done upon his knees.

RUDYARD KIPLING

A garden is a welcome distraction, our opportunity to make a detour into the world of intense color to bring brightness to our eyes, fresh aromas to cleanse our sense of smell and a reminder that there is new life continually bursting forth.

I may not enter the garden,
    Though I know the road thereto;
And morn by morn to the gateway
    I see the children go.

They bring back light on their faces;
    But they cannot bring back to me
What the lilies say to the roses,
    Or the songs of the butterflies be.

FRANCIS TURNER PALGRAVE

What wondrous life is this I lead!
Ripe apples drop about my head;
The luscious clusters of the vine
Upon my mouth do crush their wine;
The nectarine, and curious peach,
Into my hands themselves do reach;
Stumbling on melons, as I pass,
Ensnared with flowers, I fall on grass.

ANDREW MARVELL

$\mathcal{I}$f I could put my woods in song,
    And tell what's there enjoyed,
    All men would to my gardens throng,
    And leave the cities void.

RALPH WALDO EMERSON

One summer day
I chanced to stray
To a garden of flowers blooming wild.
It took me once more
To the dear days of yore
And a spot that I loved as a child.

There were the phlox,

Tall hollyhocks,

Violets perfuming the air,

Frail eglantines,

Shy columbines,

And marigolds everywhere....

COLE PORTER

I mind me in the days departed,
How often underneath the sun
With childish bounds I used to run
To a garden long deserted....

I called the place my wilderness,
For no one entered there but I;
The sheep looked in, the grass to espy,
And passed it ne'ertheless.

The trees were interwoven wild,
And spread their boughs enough about
To keep both sheep and shepherd out,
　　But not a happy child.

Adventurous joy it was for me!
I crept beneath the boughs, and found
A circle smooth of mossy ground
　　Beneath a poplar tree.

Elizabeth Barrett Browning

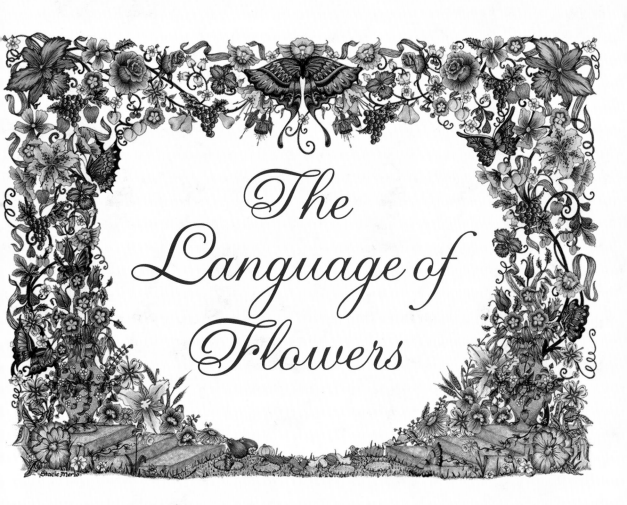

The Language of Flowers

$\mathcal{R}$ain do not hurt my flowers,
  but quickly spread
Your honey drops: press not to smell
  them here:
When they are ripe, their odour will ascend
And at your lodging with their thanks appear.

GEORGE HERBERT

The rose is a sign of joy and love,

    Young blushing love in its earliest dawn;

And the mildness that suits the gentle dove,

    From the myrtle's snowy flower is drawn.

Innocence shines in the lily's bell,

    Pure as the heart in its native heaven;

Fame's bright star and glory's swell,

    By the glossy leaf of the bay are given.

The silent soft and humble heart,
    In the violet's hidden sweetness breathes;
And the tender soul that cannot part,
    A twine of evergreen fondly wreathes...

Then, gather a wreath from the garden bowers,
And tell the wish of thy heart in flowers.

JAMES GATES PERCIVAL

What a desolate place
would be a world without flowers.
It would be a face without
a smile; a feast without
a welcome.

CLARA L. BALFOUR

The buttercup is like a golden cup,

    The marigold is like a golden frill,

The daisy with a golden eye looks up,

    And golden spreads the flag beside the rill,

    And gay and golden nods the daffodil,

The gorsey common swells a golden sea,
  The cowslip hangs a head of golden tips,
And golden drips the honey which the bee
  Sucks from sweet hearts of flowers and
    stores and sips.

CHRISTINA ROSSETTI

Flowers are the messengers for the most significant events of our lives. A tiny, simple rosebud in a church pulpit announces the arrival of a new life. A corsage for the special dance or anniversary conveys the feelings of fondness and love the giver holds for you. The grand display of bouquets at a wedding join in the festive celebration of two becoming one.

The plant or cut flowers sent to the hospital room implies concern as well as encouragement. The abundance of floral arrangements at a memorial service often reflects the significance of one's life and deeds.

Isn't it interesting how flowers welcome our entrance into life and then accompany our departure. What would we do if there were no gardens?

With little here to do or see
Of things that in the great world be,
Daisy! again I talk to thee,
For thou art worthy;
Thou unassuming commonplace
Of Nature, with that homely face,
And yet with something of a grace
Which love make for thee!

WILLIAM WORDSWORTH

Flowers. What do they do? They remind us there is more to life than work. They slow us down, activate the senses, pull out long-forgotten memories, liven up the dullest of gatherings, bring a new meaning into what may have been a drab day.

Still from the far-off pastures comes the bee,
And swings all day inside the holly hock,
Or steals her honey from the winged sweet-pea,
Or the striped glory of the four-o'clock;
The pale sweet-william, ringed with pink and white,
Grows yet within the damp shade of the wall;

And there the primrose stands, that as the night
Begins to gather, and the dews to fall,
Flings wide to circling moths her twisted buds,
That shine like yellow moons with pale, cold glow,
And all the air her heavy fragrance floods,
And gives largess to any winds that blow.

MARGARET DELAND

Flowers have their own language. Theirs is an oratory that speaks in perfumed silence, and there is tenderness, and passion, and even the lightheartedness of mirth, in the variegated beauty of their vocabulary....No spoken word can approach the delicacy of sentiment to be inferred from a flower seasonably offered; the

softest expressions may be thus conveyed without
offense, and even profound grief alleviated, at a
moment when the most tuneful voice would grate
harshly on the ear, and when the stricken soul
can be soothed only by unbroken silence.

HARVEY GAIL

There has fallen a splendid tear
    From the passion-flower at the gate.
She is coming, my dove, my dear;
    She is coming, my life, my fate.
The red rose cries, "She is near, she is near";
    And the white rose weeps, "She is late";
The larkspur listens, "I hear, I hear";
    And the lily whispers, "I wait."

ALFRED, LORD TENNYSON

The hyacinth purple, and white, and blue,

Which flung from its bells a sweet peal anew

Of music, so delicate, soft, and intense,

It was felt like an odor within the sense.

PERCY BYSSHE SHELLEY

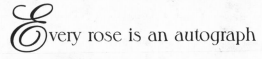

$\mathscr{E}$very rose is an autograph

from the hand of God.

THEODORE PARKER

$\mathcal{D}$eep within a shady dell
violets ever hiding.
Take them now, and let them tell
of friendship all abiding.
So may joys
shine forth today,
shedding fragrance on your way.

ELLIS WALTON

How could such sweet and
Wholesome hours
Be reckoned but with
Herbs and flowers?

ANDREW MARVELL

Pluck not the wayside flower!
It is the traveller's dower;
A thousand passers-by
Its beauties may espy,
May win a touch of blessing
From Nature's mild caressing.
The sad of heart perceives
A violet under leaves,
Like some fresh-budding hope;

The primrose on the slope
A spot of sunshine dwells,
And cheerful message tells
Of kind renewing power.
The nodding bluebell's dye
Is drawn from happy sky.
Then spare the wayside flower!
It is the traveller's dower.

ANONYMOUS

Through the open windows also,
at almost any time of the year,
pours the delicious scent of leaf
and flower—of winter sweet, violets,
or sweet peas; of stocks, or
mignonette, of wallflowers, or roses....
These, and a hundred other fragrances

mingled together in infinitely varying
combinations, give sensuous joys which
even the most jaded can but appreciate.
For there is probably no pleasure so
democratic as that which is yielded by
the fragrance of flowers and leaves.

ANONYMOUS

Queen of fragrance, lovely rose,
The beauties of thy leaves disclose!
The winter's past, the tempests fly,
Soft gales breathe gently through the sky;
The lark's sweet warbling on the wing
Salutes the gay return of spring:

The silver dews, the vernal showers,
Call forth a bloomy waste of flowers;
The joyous fields, the shady woods,
Are cloth'd with green, or swell with buds;
They haste thy beauties to disclose,
Queen of fragrance, lovely rose!

WILLIAM BROOME

That shy plant—the lily of the vale,

That loves the ground,

and from the sun withholds

Her pensive beauty,

from the breeze her sweets.

WILLIAM WORDSWORTH

For to have complete satisfaction from flowers you must have time to spend with them. There must be rapport. I talk to them and they talk to me.

PRINCESS GRACE OF MONACO

The choicest buds in Flora's train,
    let other fingers twine;
Let others snatch the damask rose, or wreath
    the eglantine;
I'd leave the sunshine and parterre, and seek the
    woodland glade,
To stretch me on the fragrant bed of blue-bells
    in the shade.
Let others cull the daffodil, the lily soft and fair;
And deem the tulip's gaudy cup most beautiful and rare;

But give to me, oh, give to me the coronal that's made
Of ruby orchids mingled with the blue-bells in the shade.
The sunflower and the peony, the poppy bright and gay,
Have no alluring charms for me, I'd fling them all away;
Exotic bloom may fill the vase, or grace the
     high-born maid;
But sweeter far to me than all, are blue-bells in the shade.

ELIZA COOK

Pansies! Pansies! How I love you, pansies!

Jaunty-faced, laughing-lipped and

dewy-eyed with glee;

Would my song but blossom in little

five-leaf stanzas

As delicate in fancies

As your beauty to me!

JAMES WHITCOMB RILEY

All night have the roses heard
The flute, violin, bassoon;
All night has the casement jessamine stirred
To the dancers dancing in tune;
Till a silence fell with the waking bird,
And a hush with the setting moon.

ALFRED, LORD TENNYSON

Flowers and seasons are inseparable.
Each season brings a changing array
of color, form, and fragrance. And
every flower brings alive memories
of similar seasons long past while
hailing new experiences to enrich
the present stage of our life.

Come into the autumn of the year—a time
when your eyes are taken by the muted,
hazy sights of gentle, softer tones, which
can then burst into vivid reds and oranges.
It has been called the "season of mists and
mellow fruitfulness." In many ways it is the

climax of the journey of colors before they fade to the dormant time of winter. Autumn–the time of year which leaves you with real expression of color to last until they emerge again in the spring.

J. BARRY FERGUSON AND TOM COWAN

*E*ach year there is a song. It is the song of the coming again of spring. Its melody reflects the bursting forth of an array of colors—especially as reflected in the yellow, mauve, purple and white.

Hundreds of them are smiling up,

Each with a flame in its shining cup

By the touch of the warm and

welcome sun

Opened suddenly. Spring's begun!

CICELY MARY BARKER

At Christmas I no more desire a rose

Than wish a snow in May's

new-fangled mirth;

But like of each thing that in season grows.

SHAKESPEARE

In those vernal seasons of the year,
when the air is calm and pleasant,
it were an injury and sullenness against Nature
not to go out, and see her riches, and partake
in her rejoicing with Heaven and Earth.

JOHN MILTON

So then the year is repeating its old story again. We are come once more, thank God! to its most charming chapter. The violets and the May flowers are as its inscriptions or vignettes. It always makes a pleasant impression on us, when we open again at these pages of the book of life.

JOHANN WOLFGANG VON GOETHE

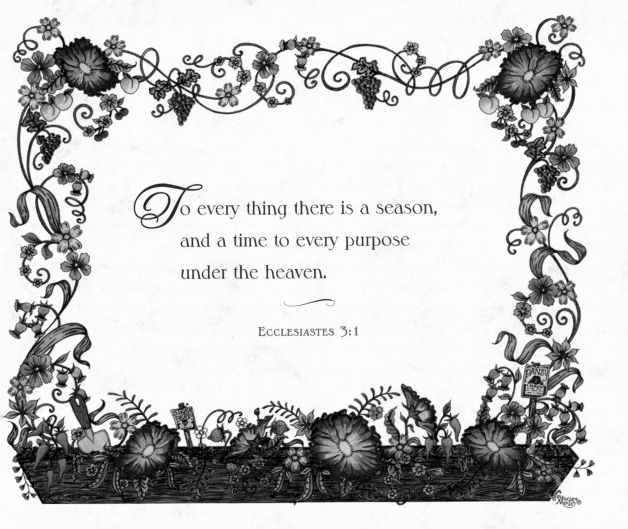

To every thing there is a season, and a time to every purpose under the heaven.

ECCLESIASTES 3:1

A sensitive plant in a garden grew,
And the young winds fed it with
silver dew,
And it opened its fan-like leaves
to the light,
And closed them beneath
the kisses of night.

And the spring arose on the garden fair,
Like the Spirit of Love felt every where;
And each flower and herb on Earth's
 dark breast
Rose from the dreams of its wintry rest.

PERCY BYSSHE SHELLEY

For lo, the winter is past,
the rain is over and gone;
The flowers appear on the earth,
the time of singing has come,
And the voice of the turtledove
is heard in our land.

THE SONG OF SOLOMON

Therefore all seasons shall be sweet to thee,
Whether the summer clothe the general earth
With greenness, or the redbreast sit and sing
Betwixt the tufts of snow on the bare branch
Of mossy apple-tree, while the nigh thatch
Smokes in the sun-thaw; whether the
    eave-drops fall

Heard only in the trances of the blast,
Or if the secret ministry of frost
Shall hang them up in silent icicles,
Quietly shining to the quiet moon.

SAMUEL TAYLOR COLERIDGE

As the flowers of spring give witness
to the departure of winter, their message
is one we all long to hear—one
of rebirth, renewal, and resurrection.
They invite us to once again
experience the freshness of life itself.
What a welcome invitation!

May the beauty of the Lord be upon you
and establish the work of your hands.

CREDITS

The quote by J. Barry Ferguson and Tom Cowan is adapted from
Living With Flowers (New York: Rizzoli, 1990).

The quote by Harvey Gail is from *The Language of Flowers*
(New York: Gramercy Books, Avenel, 1995).

Scripture quotations are from the King James Version.

Harvest House Publishers and H. Norman Wright have made
every effort to trace the ownership of all copyrighted poems and obtain
permission for their use. In the event of any question arising from the use
of any poem or quote, we regret any error made and will be pleased to
make the necessary correction in future editions of this book.